To My Children

Who have stood by me with
patience and prayer — ever
letting me draw from their
strength by their constant love
and concern.

Text copyright © MCMLXXXIV by Dorene Waggoner
Art copyright © MCMLXXXIV by The C.R. Gibson Company
Published by The C.R. Gibson Company
Norwalk, Connecticut 06856
ISBN 0-8378-2040-5

The author wishes to thank the National Council of the Churches
of Christ in the U.S.A. for use of Bible quotes from the Revised
Standard Version of the Bible, copyrighted 1946, 1952, © 1971, 1973.

I Will Not Leave You Comfortless

By
Dorene Waggoner

Illustrated by Kazue Mizumura

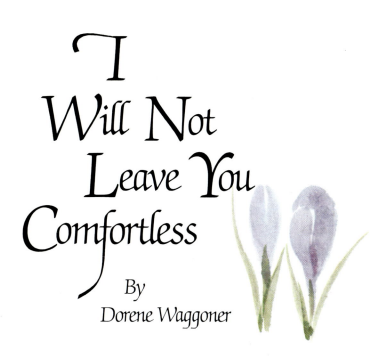

The C.R. Gibson Company, Norwalk, Connecticut 06856

Introduction

If you have begun reading this book, you are probably now facing or already have been confronted with the shattering loss of a loved one. It is a loss that is almost insurmountable. I, too, have experienced such a loss.

I battled an unending war against the inevitable. My battle cry was a resounding echo of my inability to accept the loss of the man who had been my husband for 22 years. I found myself fighting against God, crying loudly of unjust treatment.

Time and again I had tried to give it all over to God, to say truly, "Thy will be done," but I could not. I read of others who quietly accepted God's will. Their strength, faith and endurance screamed at me of how weak I must be. They seemed to find greater inner peace through death, yet I was crying my rebellion.

When I became too weary to take one battle step further, God, in his unending love and patience, gently lifted me onto a plateau. It was an often wavering smoothness, but it was a place in my life where I could catch my breath and slow my heartbeat. A place to pause — to look inside my heart and catch a glimmer of God's love and continuous support. He touched me, ever so quietly, and whispered, "Be still, and know that I am here."

The fog before my eyes slowly began to lift and again I dimly saw God's beauty and miracles around me and in all of us. Once more I began counting my blessings — not sorrows — and I was able to feel praise in place of anguish. I knew there were still valleys to cross but now I could see the hazy forms of the mountain tops beyond. Slowly and miraculously I was beginning the long journey of acceptance.

Throughout my journey, I found sustenance in writing down my deepest thoughts and prayers to God. Somehow, these words returned to me, and I felt helped. On sleepless nights, verses from the Bible would come to me with a whole new meaning — reaching out, it seemed, to touch my soul — and I would write them down and return to them again and again.

My prayer, my only aim in writing this book is that somehow my words and the words of Scripture that helped me may help someone else who is fighting the same battle for strength, courage and hope. The circumstances will differ but the stages of rebellion, fear, anger and anguish probably will not. It is a long journey but be of good faith. You are not alone. There is peace in the healing balm of God's love. He will not leave you comfortless.

D. W.

To Whom Much is Given . . .

Gradually, but ever so gradually, my mind is accepting that prayers are answered in different ways. How much easier it is to say to someone else that the death of a loved one is God's will. How much harder it is to accept it yourself.

My anger at myself, my weakness, is giving way to peace. I began letting myself go, my self-blame go, my doubts and fears go, and slowly God is becoming real to me again. I am beginning to realize, as Luke 12:48 says, "Every one to whom much is given, of him will much be required."

I have been given so much, Lord.

Help me to realize that nowhere does the Bible teach that Christians are exempt from pain and sorrow, but that through your power, you will give us courage to bear it. Help me to go beyond my afflictions and trials and look toward the glory reserved for us in heaven.

I consider that the sufferings of this present time are not worth comparing with the glory that is to be revealed to us.

Romans 8:18

According to Your Plan, Lord

How often I have cried to you and felt I was not heard. In distress I cried, wanting only one way — my way. As a child I cried and would not listen. Help me, O Lord, to listen always, help me to reach and know that you are there all the time waiting to console.

Lord, help me to listen so that I may hear all that you so lovingly wish to bestow. In my desperation, I could not accept your will for my beloved. I loved him so much — he was my life.

Help me to accept what I cannot change — to accept your will and to grow in strength and patience. Help me to bear my loneliness with grace and confidence.

We know that in everything
God works for good with those
who love him, who are called
according to his purpose.

Romans 8:28

Everything moves according to your plan, and our time
on earth is short. Help me to use it wisely. May I realize
I have no strength within myself. I tried with all my
strength to make my loved one well — to make him
whole again. But with all my strength I failed. My
strength was for naught in comparison to your will for
his life.

What is your life? For you are a
mist that appears for a little
time and then vanishes.

James 4:14

The Answer to Sorrow

I am finding that Christ is the answer to sorrow.
Though I called him, I had my back turned to him and I
felt he was not listening. As we walk through the valley
of the shadow of death, as we say goodbye to those we
love, as we suffer loneliness and misery, darkness and
despair, Christ will be with us if we but let him.

In my sorrow, Lord Jesus, may your comfort take all
the bitterness and longing away and give me courage to
face my heartache. Through your grace, I will be con-
soled and by your arms I will be supported. Thank you
dear Lord.

In my distress I called upon the
Lord; to my God I cried for help.
From his temple he heard my
voice, and my cry to him
reached his ears.

Psalms 18:6

May I commit my burden of guilt and distress to you, Lord? Help me to walk patiently in your way with the assurance that your will in my life will be done.

Help me to do away with anger and impatience. I will take my rest in you, Lord.

Come to me, all who labor and are heavy-laden, and I will give you rest.

Matthew 11:28

I Will Wait upon Thee, Lord

Although I do not understand now, Lord, give me patience to wait for total understanding, for total knowledge. Help me not to trouble myself trying to find the answers — for my heart knows they will not come in this lifetime. Let it be enough that you will guide my path and lead, if I will but let you.

For now we see in a mirror
dimly, but then face to face.
Now I know in part; then I
shall understand fully, even as I
have been fully understood.

I Corinthians 13:12

Be still before the Lord, and
wait patiently for him.

Psalms 37:7

Let me keep you in the center of my will. I pray I will
always give you the honor and the glory. Help me to
trust with all my heart and never rely on my own
insight. Lead me to a new understanding of your com-
mandments, to a new awareness of your will for my life.

In all your ways acknowledge
him, and he will make straight
your paths.

Proverbs 3:6

Keep My Mind on You, Lord

Keep my mind on you, Lord, and help me to discipline myself and my thoughts that so often crowd out your peace. Let me live close to you, Lord Jesus, that your wisdom will continually prevail in my mind.

Whatever I fear the most, Lord, I will put into your loving hands, knowing that you will give me peace and courage, calmness and strength. Thank you for the peace you have given me which does not depend on feelings or circumstances.

Thou dost keep him in perfect peace, whose mind is stayed on thee, because he trusts in thee.

Isaiah 26:3

May my meditation be pleasing to you, O Lord. I will seek your presence always through my prayers. Purify my thoughts continually by the cleansing power of your Holy Spirit, Lord.

I will remember your overflowing goodness to me and my family. Your gentle mercy with my beloved — to ease him of pain and remove all fear. For your ever abiding presence I praise you and will continually give you thanksgiving.

Let the words of my mouth and the meditation of my heart be acceptable in thy sight, O Lord, my rock and my redeemer.

Psalms 19:14

At Times I Falter, Lord

How I yearn for you, Lord, but so often my heart is drawn away from your leading. I am again caught up in sadness and loneliness. Help me, O Lord, for I long for your fellowship. Help me not to turn away from your love.

In times of weakness may I learn to say, from the deepest recesses of my heart — "Thy will be done." I want to stop asking, to listen and search and learn your will in my life. Lift me from the low vale of selfishness to the high plain of creativeness with you, my Heavenly father.

… the Spirit helps us in our weakness; for we do not know how to pray as we ought, but the Spirit himself intercedes for us with sighs too deep for words.

Romans 8:26

It is comforting to know that all my needs, not all my wants, will be supplied from your abundant storehouse. Thank you for giving me your peace that passes all understanding, that I may rejoice in you even in my lonely hours. Help me to have no anxiety about anything, but to rely on your abundant goodness to care for it all.

I will come to you Lord, when my steps falter, for you are my hope, my joy, my peace. Through your love, my hope will once again renew and joy will return to my life.

And my God will supply every need of yours according to his riches in glory in Christ Jesus.

Phillipian's 4:19

Let My Trials be of Use

From this sorrow that has come to my life, let me use it to help others know about you. May I see the needs around me and be willing to serve you in the way you have chosen. Give me an open mind and heart and let me be filled with your knowledge, your goodness and love.

Help me, Father, to realize that you do not make mistakes. That your way is the perfect way that leads to everlasting joy. You touch our lives with your gentle hand to mold and make us useful vessels if we but give ourselves over to your will and your way.

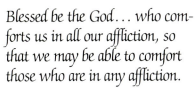

Blessed be the God... who comforts us in all our affliction, so that we may be able to comfort those who are in any affliction.

2 Corinthians 1:3,4

Thank you, Lord, for helping me remove the pain from my heart. Perhaps a void, an emptiness, will always remain, but help me to learn to live with it. Show me how to compensate for this. Help me learn to do something constructive, something to help others. This will perhaps ease the loneliness and make me feel whole again.

Now may our Lord Jesus Christ himself, and God our Father, who loved us and gave us eternal comfort and good hope through grace, comfort your hearts and establish them in every good work and word.

2 Thessalonians 2:16-17

God is for Us:

God is for us! He did not promise us joy always. He does not always feel joy. He gave us his only Son! Thank you, God, for your most precious gift. Thank you for preparing a way — for preparing a place for my beloved. I know someday we will be together again in perfect love.

    I claim your promise to be with me always. I pray I will seek your will and your way in all my life. Help me to know that no matter how dark and lonely I am, you will be with me — my rock and my shield.

If God is for us, who is against us? He who did not spare his own Son, but gave him up for us all, will he not also give us all things with him?

Romans 8:32–33

Help me to stand firm without fear, to acknowledge you as my light and my salvation, to witness without fear. May I never forget that you are the strength of my life and I can do nothing from my own power.

My heart and soul praises you, my Redeemer, for the light that dispels my deepest gloom and transforms my life with your unselfish love and tender care.

The Lord is my light and my
salvation; whom shall I fear?
The Lord is the stronghold of my
life; of whom shall I be afraid?

Psalms 27:1

A Shield about Me

Thank you, Lord, for removing my sleepless nights, for giving me the contentment to lie down to a quiet sleep. Thank you for removing the awesome visions of my nightmares and helping me feel at peace with myself in the memory of my beloved. May I ever lift up my head in thanksgiving for your gentle touch, for your supporting arms when my loneliness and fear again begin to overcome me.

But thou, O Lord, art a shield
about me, my glory, and the
lifter of my head... I lie down
and sleep; I wake again, for the
Lord sustains me. I am not
afraid.

Psalms 3:3,5,6

The greatness of your love overwhelms me. Thank you, Lord Jesus, for being patient with me in my trials. Though I felt so alone, so empty — thank you for never giving up, for not turning your back on me.

Help me to arise each morning realizing that it is your day. May I always thank you for a new sunrise, for a night without fear.

May the God of hope fill you
with all joy and peace in believ-
ing, so that by the power of the
Holy Spirit you may abound in
hope.

Romans 15:13

How Wondrous is Your Love:

Oh Lord, how small we are in comparison to your great and wondrous universe, and yet you have crowned us with honor and glory. You have made us your own. You have created us special and apart in your own image, bearing eternal souls. How wondrous is your love! How humbly do I bow at the majesty of your greatness.

Your care is from everlasting to everlasting, your love excels all excellence, all description. Thank you for the morning of hope, for the awareness of your abundant goodness and tender mercies.

When I look at thy heavens, the work of thy fingers, the moon and the stars which thou hast established; what is man that thou art mindful of him, and the son of man that thou dost care for him?

Psalms 8:3-4

Let the balm of your peace pour over me and I will humbly praise you, Almighty God. Thank you for the peace that is washing my soul clean and filling me with a desire of newness, a joy for living in this beautiful world that has been created and given to us.

The steadfast love of the Lord
never ceases, his mercies never
come to an end; they are new
every morning.

Lamentations 3:22-23

A New Sunrise

I will see my beloved again in the land of the living.
Make my way straight, Lord, and help me to wait on
you and not run ahead. Give my heart courage and let it
be stronger than my mind. Only in our hearts can we
fully accept loss and understand grief.

    Through my tears I am washing my heart and seeing
you more clearly. I think of your anguish, your heart-
break, as your only Son hung on the cross. This small
glimmer helps me bear my loss a little better.

I believe that I shall see the
goodness of the Lord in the land
of the living! Wait for the Lord;
be strong, and let your heart
take courage.

Psalms 27:13-14

Thank you for the blessing of your Son. Thank you for the sunrise of the resurrection. Help me, Lord, to remember the need to rejoice in you continually; to go beyond circumstance, no matter how desperate or sorrowful, and see you as my hope and joy. May I daily reach out to you and be filled with your everlasting love.

... and that Christ may dwell in your hearts through faith; that you, being rooted and grounded in love, may have power to comprehend with all the saints what is the breadth and length and height and depth, and to know the love of Christ which surpasses knowledge, that you may be filled with all the fullness of God.

Ephesians 3:17-19

Designed by Patrice Barrett
Type set in Zapf Chancery